Big Sur
and the
Central Coast

Big Sur and the Central Coast

Photography by
David Muench

Introduction by
Jeffrey Whitmore

SKYLINE
PRESS

Produced by Boulton Publishing Services, Toronto
Designed by Fortunato Aglialoro

© 1984 Chicago Review Press
SKYLINE PRESS is an imprint of Chicago Review Press

ISBN 1-55652-045-X, previously ISBN 0-19-540605-2
Printed in Hong Kong by Everbest Printing Company, LTD.,
through Four Colour Imports, LTD.

INTRODUCTION ———————————————————

On my first visit to the Central Coast I stayed the night in a tiny board-and-batten cabin in the Monterey Peninsula town of Pacific Grove. After dinner that evening, I strolled to nearby Lovers Point, a rocky promontory that juts into Monterey Bay. Runners of fog made their way up the street and crept in among the other cabins huddled together on either side of the way. A foghorn moaned in the distance, punctuation to the rhythmic crashing of sea against shore. The scent of pine trees and sea air was borne on the wisps of fog. Mingling of sea and pine, crash of wave, foghorn's moan—all was redolent of my boyhood on the New England coast.

This was not California, I felt. This was Nantucket, Gloucester, Martha's Vineyard, Cape Cod...this was home.

The feeling was not original with me. Robert Louis Stevenson, after traveling about the Central Coast in the late nineteenth century, observed: 'Such scenes are very similar in different climates; they appear homely to the eyes of all; to me this was like a dozen spots in Scotland.'

The Central Coast, which, roughly speaking, stretches from the Monterey Bay south through Big Sur to San Luis Obispo Bay, offers such a variety of environments to visitors that it is not surprising each can find some aspect of his homeland here.

To the south, the monolithic guardian rock at Morro Bay looms above the sea with the physical presence of Mont-Saint-Michel (it has the mystical force of a Magritte painting); heading north, the serpentine stretch of Highway 1 that clings to the Santa Lucia range, high above the blue Pacific and its foaming surf line, might be mistaken for the road that twists above the Mediterranean between Salerno and Positano; to a Kentucky mountain man, the rugged wilderness of Big Sur might seem like home, and the rugged individualists who inhabit it like kin; the grottoes of Point Lobos are reminiscent of those one might explore on some Grecian isle (and for lovers of literary adventure, reminiscent of *Treasure Island*, which was partially inspired by Stevenson's wanderings on that dramatic spit of land); a traveler on the Monterey–Salinas highway might look up to the grassy, oak-dotted slopes at the Basque shepherds tending their flocks and think himself transported to the Pyrenees.

Perhaps only the ghost of Mad Ludwig of Bavaria could feel at home in the most extravagant dwelling ever constructed on the Central Coast—La Casa Grande at San Simeon. With its 150-foot-high twin towers rising from the slopes of the Santa Lucias, the Spanish-Moorish castle of the late newspaper baron William Randolph Hearst encompasses a trove of art and architecture garnered from every corner of the world. It is a monument to opulence and garishness; it is exquisite and gauche. In *Citizen Kane*, the classic movie loosely based on Hearst's life, this fabulous homestead is called Xanadu, after the 'stately pleasure dome' in Coleridge's *Kubla Khan*. During its heyday, in the late twenties and early thirties, the estate was visited by such notables as Winston Churchill, George Bernard Shaw, Charles Lindbergh, and Charlie Chaplin. The guest list was exclusive, and an invitation from Hearst was considered a measure of status, particularly for members of the Hollywood film colony. Today the estate is part of California's state park system and is officially designated 'Hearst San Simeon State Historical Monument'. Each year nearly a million visitors walk the hallways and corridors once reserved for the great and the near great.

Archaeological evidence suggests that the first visitors to the Central Coast were hunters who came here 10,000 years ago in search of game. Some 2,500 years later, another wave of visitors arrived and stayed to make their home here. They lived on nuts, seeds, and berries, which they gathered in the fields and forests, and on the shellfish and other bounty they collected from rocky ledges, reefs, and tidepools along the coast. Their descendants—American Indians of the Costanoan group—were still living that way when the first Europeans arrived at the beginning of the seventeenth century.

Sebastián Vizcaíno, a Portuguese navigator in the employ of Spain, landed on the Central Coast in 1602 and explored what is now Monterey and Carmel. Although he sent back a glowing report—the harbor was a 'noble harbor' and the climate resembled that of Castile—Spain took little notice. More than a century and a half would pass before another European visited the Central Coast.

When Gaspar de Portolá and Father Junípero Serra arrived in Monterey in 1770 they wasted little time in establishing a Spanish presence. Father Serra founded Mission San Carlos Borromeo de Monterey (which he moved next year to Carmel and re-named Mission San Carlos Borromeo de Carmelo) and began converting the Indians to the Catholic faith. Thus began a 75-year period of Spanish-Mexican rule in California, and thus ended the traditional Costanoan culture.

The missions were the focal point of life in California until 1834, when the Mexican government—which had declared its independence from Spain in 1822—ordered them secularized. They soon fell into disrepair and eventual ruin. However, thanks in large part to a remarkable man named Harry Downie who sparked a mission revival in the 1930s, most of them have been restored.

Of historical interest today, the missions are also a living part of community life on the Central Coast. Music was always important in the mission system— a giant hand with musical notations on it is painted on the wall at Mission San Antonio de Padua near Jolon—and still it reverberates vitally within the resurrected structures. Each year at Christmas time, throngs of music lovers fill the basilicas at Mission San Carlos Borromeo de Carmelo and Mission San Juan Bautista, as the past is infused with life through the timeless magic of Vivaldi, Corelli, and Bach.

The Mexican occupation of California lasted about twenty years, ending when war broke out between Mexico and the United States and Commodore John D. Sloat raised the American flag over the Custom House in Monterey on 7 July 1846.

One of the first cultural contributions of the Yankees was the establishment of the Union Theater in Jack Swan's saloon. The adobe stands today as 'California's First Theatre' (sic), and audiences still hiss the villains and cheer the heroines in such classic melodramas as *Ruined by Drink* and *Lady Audley's Secret*.

Monterey served as provisional capital of the California Territory until a constitutional convention met there in 1849 to draft a state constitution. The constitution once drafted and with statehood on the way, the capital was moved from Monterey to San Jose and thence to Sacramento, where it now is located.

Having lost its political importance—as well as much of its population, who had departed for the gold fields of the Mother Lode—Monterey slid into a decline that endured until 1880 and the opening of the Del Monte Hotel. As the hotel began to prosper, Monterey acquired a new industry, which persists to this day—tourism. As Del Monte Properties grew over the years—particularly under the guidance of Samuel F. B. Morse—Pebble Beach, with its scenic 17-Mile Drive and internationally acclaimed golf courses, became a symbol of the good life. But not only sightseers and golfers were attracted to the area.

The fishery of Monterey Bay has drawn people from all over the world. Chinese fishermen once dried their catch on the shores of Pacific Grove, while their countrymen worked side by side with the Portuguese whalers of Carmel and Point Lobos. (The remains of a whaler's cottage still stand at Point Lobos not far from the rocky shores where viewers gather each year to observe the migration of the California gray whale.)

After the turn of the century, Pietro Ferrante, a transplanted Sicilian fisherman, revolutionized the Monterey fishing industry by introducing the *lampara* net. It enabled fishermen to catch more fish faster than ever before and it brought to Monterey an influx of Italian fishermen with their families whose influence—politically, culturally, and economically—is a major force in the community today.

Between the maritime and tourist-oriented atmosphere of Monterey and the fantasy world of Hearst's castle at San Simeon lies Big Sur. *El pais grande del Sur*, the Spanish called it—'the big country of the South'. They saw it as unconquerable land, and they left it alone. Not until late in the nineteenth century did a few pioneer families begin to settle there (many of their descendants live there still) and not until 1937, with the opening of Highway 1 between San Simeon and Carmel, was there anything like easy access to Big Sur. Even today, mud and rock slides disrupt the flow of traffic through the area, or halt it altogether.

Something wild haunts this area, something otherworldly. Perhaps it is suggested by the infinity of misty headlands ranked along the pounding sea, or perhaps Big Sur's enchantment derives from the presence of the giant coast redwoods, *Sequoia sempervirens*. Just as the moss-bearded trees in Henry Wadsworth Longfellow's forest primeval stood 'like the Druids of eld', so these ancient redwoods stand in the canyons of Big Sur, druidic, hinting of some ancient mystery. John Steinbeck, who in his novels immortalized the prosaic doings of Monterey's Cannery Row and the Salinas Valley, once wrote that 'the vainest, most slap-happy and irreverent of men, in the presence of redwoods goes under a spell of wonder and respect'.[1]

Henry Miller, another author who found a home on the Central Coast, called this place a paradise, 'where to give thanks to the Creator comes naturally and easy'.[2]

For those of us fortunate enough to live here, the words of Steinbeck and Miller ring true. Here, where the wild sea beats against the shore, where the redwood towers in ancient majesty above the canyon floor, and where, in the high meadows of the Santa Lucia, the track of the puma can still be seen upon the land, we know we are in paradise; and in our paradise it is natural for us to feel wonder and respect and to smile unaffectedly as we offer up our thanks.

Monterey, 1984   JEFFREY WHITMORE

1 John Steinbeck, *Travels with Charley*, New York: Viking Press, 1962

2 Henry Miller, *Big Sur and the Oranges of Hieronymus Bosch*, New York: New Directions, 1957

1 Ocean flow near Granite Creek

2 Big Sur Coast

3 *(right)* California brown pelicans

4 Salmon Creek Falls, Santa Lucia Range,
Ventana Wilderness, Big Sur coast

5 *(right)* Pescadero Point, 17-Mile Drive

6 Tidal flow, Carmel

7 *(right)* Coast redwoods, *Sequoia sempervirens*, Big Sur

8 *(left)* Machete Ridge, Pinnacles

9 Point Sur headlands

10 Calla lilies, coastal creek, Big Sur
coastline north

11 *(right)* Big Sur coastline

12 *(left)* Little Sur River Canyon, Ventana Wilderness, Santa Lucia Range

13 Monterey Cypress on North Point, Point Lobos State Reserve

14 *(left)* Oak and grassland, Santa Lucia Range

15 Oak and grassland, Morro Bay

16 Live oaks, Del Rey Oaks

17 *(right)* The Custom House, Monterey, early 1820s

18 Docks at Morro Bay

19 *(right)* Big Sur River

20 Pacific breakers pound the shore

21 Oak, grass and woodlands above Salinas River Valley

22 *(left)* Bluefish Cove and Whalers Cove, Point Lobos State Reserve

23 Oak and grassland, foothills, Salinas Valley, Gabilan Range

24 *(left)* Foggy day at Oceano dunes, Pismo Beach

25 Monterey Bay shoreline at Pacific Grove

26 Fisherman's Wharf, Monterey

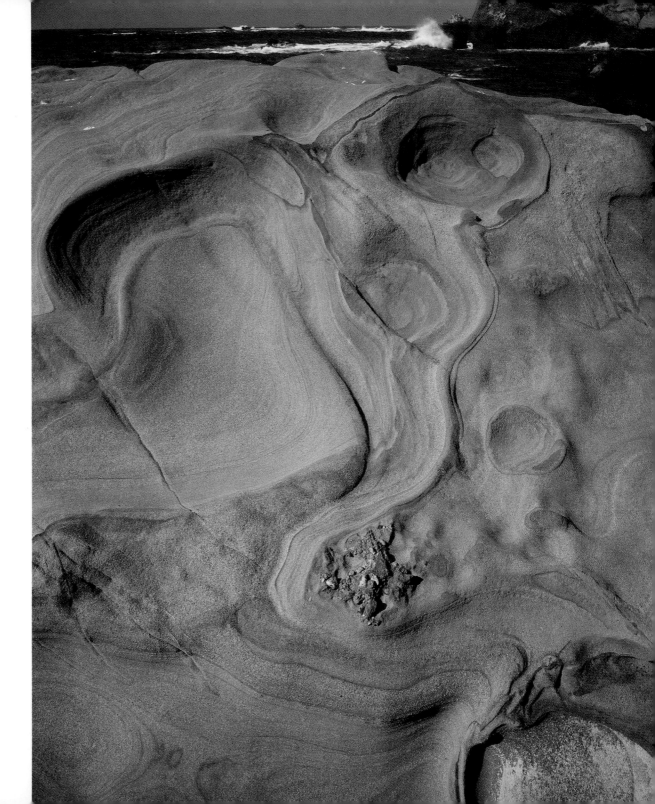

27 Sandstone formations, The Slot, Point Lobos State Reserve

28 Sunset at Pacific Grove

29 *(right)* Cannery Row, Monterey

30 The Custom House, Monterey

31 (*right*) Mission San Antonio de Padua (founded 1771), Jolon

32 Rock formation off 17-Mile Drive

33 (*right*) Courtyard fountain and belltower, Mission San Carlos Borromeo (founded 1770), Carmel

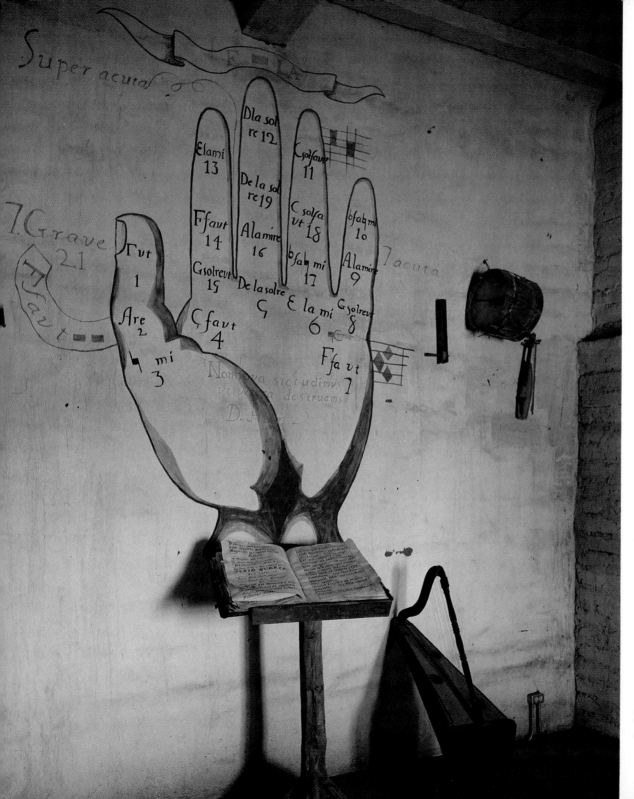

34 Musical hand of notes, Mission San
Antonio de Padua

35 Monastery door, Mission San Miguel Arcángel (*founded 1797*)

36 Casa Grande, Hearst Castle (1919–1947), San Simeon

37 Greco-Roman temple, Neptune Pool,
Hearst Castle, San Simeon

38 *(left)* Winged statuary, Neptune Pool, Hearst Castle, San Simeon

39 Roman Pool, Hearst Castle, San Simeon

40 Sequoia cones, sycamore leaf, and bay leaf, Big Sur

41 *(right)* Gothic tapestry and dining table, The Refectory, Hearst Castle, San Simeon

42 *(left)* Big Sur coast

43 Carmel River Beach State Park

44 Ranch, San Luis Valley

45 (*right*) Mission San Juan Bautista (founded 1797)

46 *(left)* View from Cypress Point, Pebble Beach, with Santa Lucia Mountains

47 Granite Creek area, Big Sur coast

48 McWay Creek waterfall, Julia Pfeiffer Burns State Park

49 *(right)* Los Laureles Grade, between Carmel Valley Road and the Monterey-Salinas Highway

50 Big Sur coast at Palo Colorado Creek

51 Seagulls, Pacific Grove

52 Morro Rock, Morro Bay

53 *(right)* Big Sur River Canyon

54 Pelicans, Morro Bay

55 Summer blossom, Big Sur coast

56 Cliff erosion, Big Sur coast

57 Big Sur coast at Garrapata Creek

58 Live oak grove, Del Rey Oaks

59 *(right)* Big Sur River Canyon

60 *(left)* Headland below Big Sur

61 Point Pinos, Pacific Grove

62 *(left)* Monterey Harbour

63 South of Big Sur

64 *(left)* Breakers, Big Sur

65 Clamming, Morro Rock

66 Cypress and bluff lettuce on granite outcrop, North Point, Point Lobos State Reserve

67 *(right)* 'California's First Theatre' *(sic)*, Monterey

68 *(left)* Century plant, Pacific Grove

69 Jellyfish, Monterey coast

70 *(left)* Monterey Cypress, Pescadero Point, 17-Mile Drive

71 Monterey Bay shoreline, Pacific Grove

72 *(left)* Pinnacle Cove, Point Lobos State Reserve

73 Sea lions on offshore rocks

74 Fog at Point Sur

75 *(right)* Surf along Big Sur coast

76 *(left)* Machete Ridge, Pinnacles

77 Coast live oak

78 Morro Rock, Morro Bay State Park

79 *(right)* Granite window, Big Sur coast

80 Poppies and erosion, Cambria

81 *(right)* Fog, Big Sur coast

82 Summer sunset, Big Sur coast

83 *(right)* Bear Gulch, Gabilan Range